MANITOWOC PUBLIC LIBRARY
JUN 16 2004
D1511227

SIMPLY SCIENCE

How Scientists Work

by Natalie M. Rosinsky

Content Adviser: Mats Selen, Ph.D.,
Department of Physics, University of Illinois at Champaign-Urbana

Science Adviser: Terrence E. Young Jr., M.Ed., M.L.S.,
Jefferson Parish (La.) Public Schools

Reading Adviser: Dr. Linda D. Labbo,
Department of Reading Education, College of Education,
The University of Georgia

COMPASS POINT BOOKS
MINNEAPOLIS, MINNESOTA

Compass Point Books
3109 West 50th Street, #115
Minneapolis, MN 55410

Visit Compass Point Books on the Internet at *www.compasspointbooks.com*
or e-mail your request to *custserv@compasspointbooks.com*

Photographs ©: Corbis, cover, 7; PhotoDisc, 4, 29; E. Schlegel/Dallas Morning News/Corbis Sygma, 5; Araldo de Luca/Corbis, 6; USDA/ARS/Scott Bauer, 9, 10, 13, 14, 16, 18, 20; Richard T. Nowitz/Corbis, 12; USDA/ARS/Brian Prechtel, 17; USDA/ARS, 21; Photo Network/Tom McCarthy, 22; Roger Ressmeyer/Corbis, 24; USDA/ARS/Keith Weller, 25; Skjold Photographs, 26; James A. Sugar/Corbis, 28; John Cross/The Free Press, 32.

Editor: Catherine Neitge
Photo Researchers: Svetlana Zhurkina and Marcie C. Spence
Designer/Page Production: Bradfordesign, Inc./The Design Lab

Library of Congress Cataloging-in-Publication Data
Rosinsky, Natalie M. (Natalie Myra)
How scientists work / by Natalie Rosinsky.
p. cm. — (Simply science)
Includes bibliographical references and index.
Contents: The world around us—Why does that happen?—Asking special questions—Learning from experiments—Repeating and sharing experiments—Taking time and thought—Using new tools.
ISBN 0-7565-0596-8 (hardcover)
1. Scientists—Juvenile literature. [1. Scientists. 2. Science—Methodology.] I. Title. II. Series: Simply science (Minneapolis, Minn.)
Q147.R67 2004
507'.2—dc22 2003014414

Printed in the United States of America.

Table of Contents

Note: In this book, words that are defined in the glossary are in ***bold*** *the first time they appear in the text.*

The World Around Us

Look around. Do you see the sun up high? Step outside and feel the wind on your face. Taste a sweet, ripe apple. Our senses give us information about the world. When milk becomes sour, it smells bad! When we hear a baby cry, we rush to help.

Our senses also raise questions. We notice changes over time. Each day, the sun seems to travel

The sun shines brightly in the sky.

A farmer stands in a field of corn ruined by lack of rain.

across the sky. Why? Some years, crops fail and there is less food to eat. Again, we ask why. We also wonder why some babies get sick and others do not. Even long ago, people asked these questions.

Why Does That Happen?

Very long ago, people made up stories to explain events. They said the sun was a god driving his golden wagon. Crops failed because an earth goddess was angry. Babies became sick when an evil person cursed them.

Such stories made people feel better. They thought prayers or offerings would bring good crops. Punishing

The Greeks of long ago thought the sun god, Helios, drove his chariot across the sky.

The Mayans of ancient Mexico believed in Chac, the rain god.

evil people would keep babies safe. They had other **superstitions** about what caused good or bad things to happen. Even today, some people are superstitious.

Scientists, of course, do not believe in superstition. When scientists ask questions, they use tools and their senses to find reasonable answers. They keep their feelings and beliefs separate from their work.

A scientist uses a microscope in his work. ▶

BAUSCH & LOMB

Asking Special Questions

Scientists ask and answer questions in a special way. It is called the scientific method. First, they spend time gathering information. They look for a pattern of things that might cause events. Will plants grow if they are watered every day? Perhaps plants will grow if people talk to them!

Scientists only use information that can be measured. How can we measure a plant's growth? We could count the number of new leaves that appear within several weeks. We could use a tool like a ruler.

Scientists use a green dye to help them study and measure rain runoff patterns.

It would show how much taller the plant has grown.

Scientists also use tools to weigh things. Other tools measure how hot or cold things are. By gathering this kind of information, scientists find a pattern. They use this pattern to form a possible answer. This answer is called a **hypothesis.** One hypothesis might be that plants grow when people talk to them daily. Scientists

Department of Agriculture scientists use a ruler to measure a plant during an experiment.

Scientists use a machine called a mass spectrometer to take measurements.

would then ask the question, "Do plants grow when people talk to them daily?"

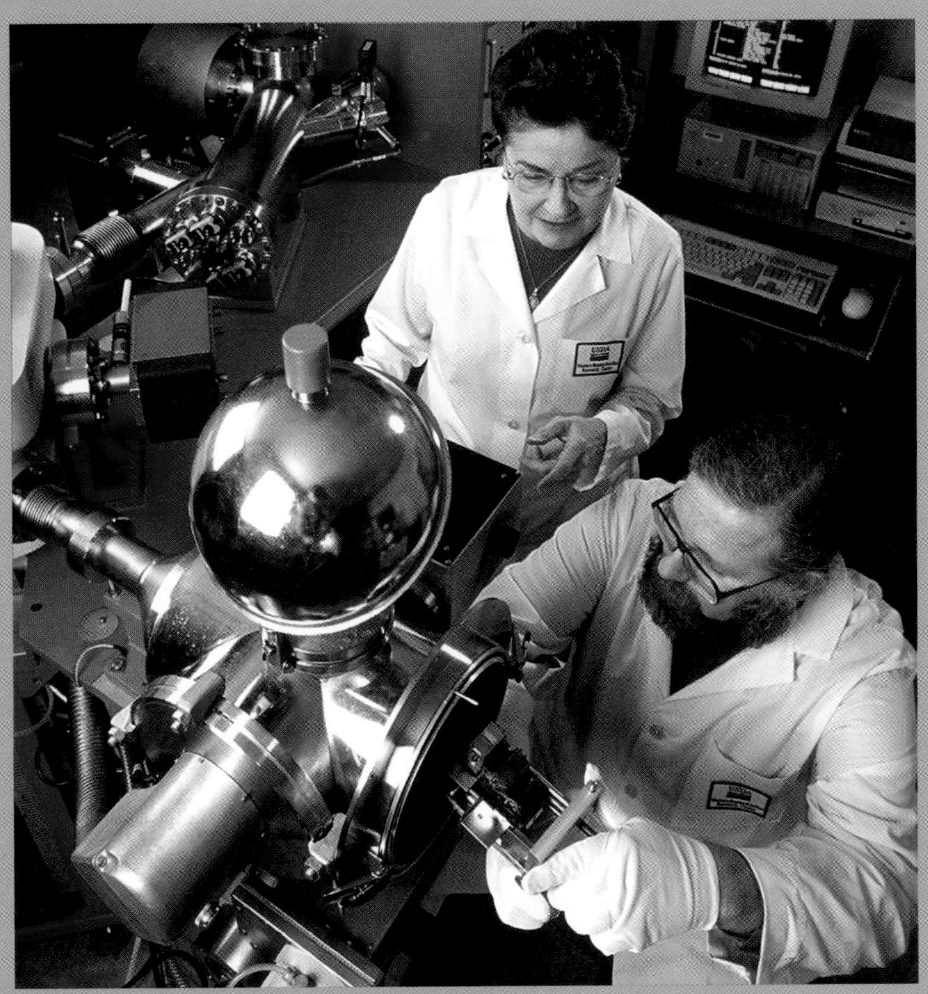

Learning from Experiments

Is a hypothesis correct? Scientists find out through experiments. In a scientific experiment, information is gathered from two different groups. One group is the test group. It could be five plants that you talk to each day. The other group is the **control group.** In this case, it would be another five plants you do not talk to. By comparing results between these groups, scientists test their hypothesis.

Scientists plan experiments carefully. They make sure test and control groups are different in only one way.

A scientist conducts an experiment with plants, straw, and a wind tunnel to study soil erosion.

For example, your two groups would use the same kind and size of plant. They would grow in the same kind and amount of soil. You would give each group the same amount of water and light. The only difference, or variable, would be the hypothesis being tested. You would talk to only one group.

Careful planning helps scientists reach their **conclusion** about a hypothesis. Limiting

After carefully planning an experiment, a scientist checks on tiny trees.

A scientist adds the exact amount of liquid to be tested.

FOLATE
METTLER
TYPE PM 300

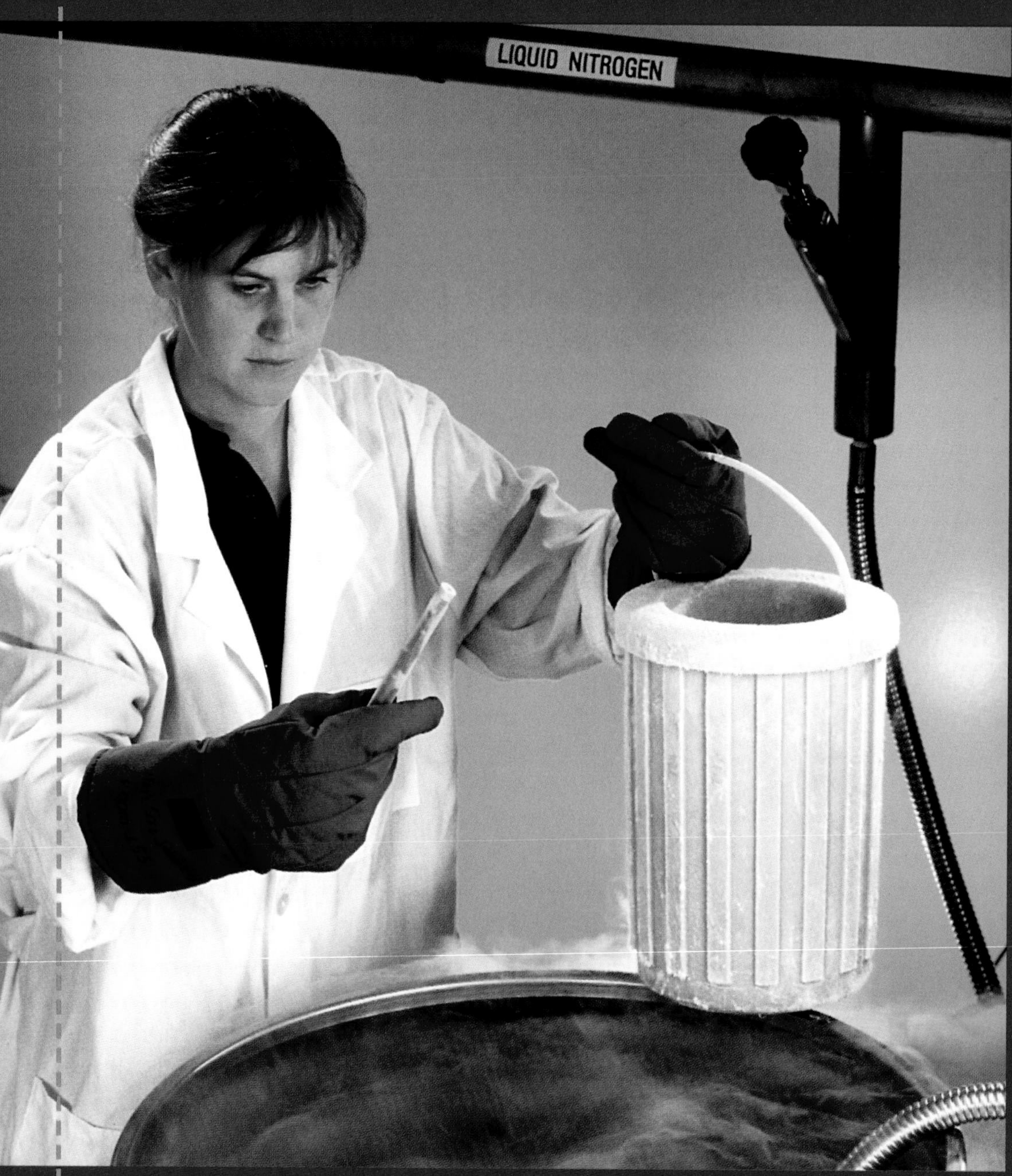
LIQUID NITROGEN

the variables helps make this conclusion a valid one. Your conclusion could be that talking to plants does help them grow. You could discover that talking to plants does not help them grow. Or, you might find out that you do not have enough **evidence** for either conclusion.

Scientists often work in teams. You could work with friends or classmates on your experiment. Scientists always take safety **precautions.** They often wear gloves and lab coats. They are very careful in their work.

A scientist wears heavy gloves and a lab coat while working with liquid nitrogen.

Repeating and Sharing Experiments

Throughout an experiment, scientists make many measurements. They keep careful records. They list each step in the experiment. Sometimes, this is the special job of one team member. You could measure your plants daily. Each day, you or a friend would write down what you saw. One of you

A chemist keeps track of soil samples in a research project.

Circled areas let the scientist measure the same spot on the mangoes at the beginning and end of an experiment.

might draw a **bar graph** showing these measurements.

Keeping careful records helps scientists repeat experiments. They want to see if the results are the same each

time. Before a conclusion is accepted by scientists, a scientist will repeat the experiment many times. Other scientists will try the experiment, too. If a conclusion is valid, the results will be the same for scientists working in

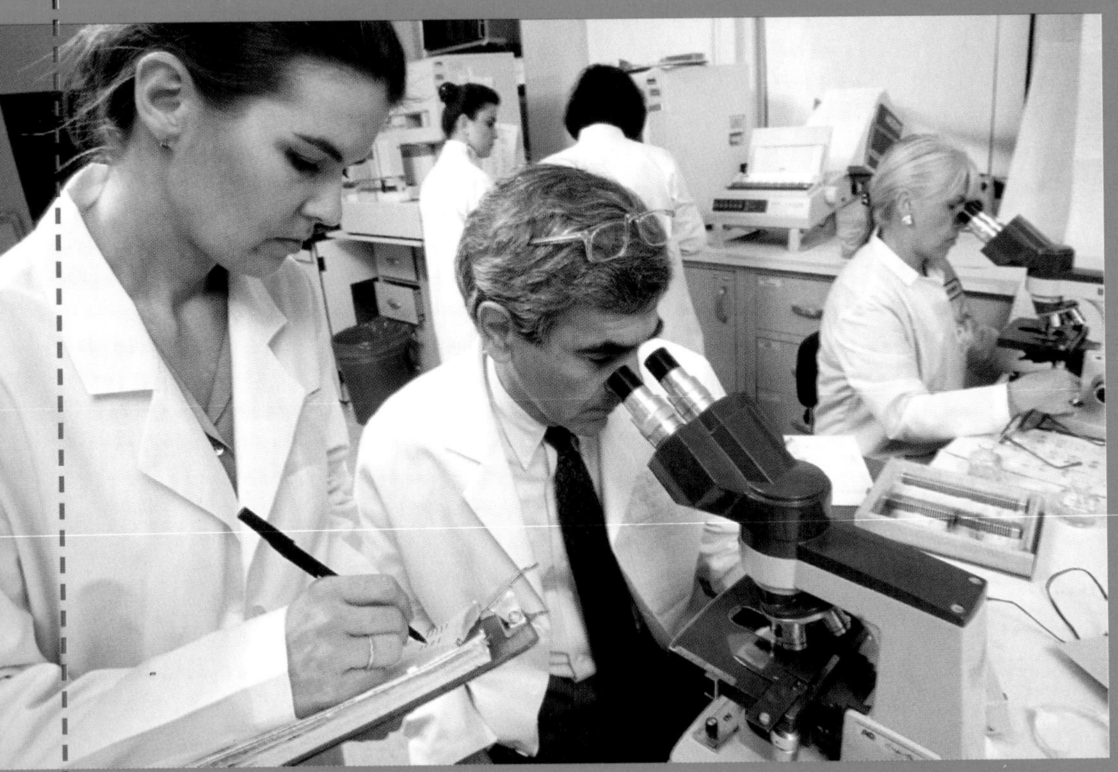

different places. Are you talking to plants in school? Try your experiment at home. Have other students try it. These are ways to check and see how valid your conclusion is.

Scientists want to know how often a hypothesis has been tested. They want to know who did these experiments. They want to see the careful records kept for each step. The best science magazines expect to receive this information. They only publish **research** results after receiving all the background information and records. Sometimes, proving that a hypothesis is wrong is useful to scientists!

Scientists keep careful records as they work.

Taking Time and Thought

Some scientists study space and the planets. Still others study the oceans. Scientists work to understand the world. They are interested in coming up with reasonable ideas that help explain what happens and why it happens. These big ideas or scientific **theories** take time and thought. Some scientists also work on ways to make everyday life better.

Scientists wear special glasses to study a 3-D map of Venus.

A scientist collects weekly water samples as part of a long research project.

Scientists may spend years on one research project. Many years may pass, too, before they can connect ideas. Using a microscope, researchers

first saw tiny germs in the 17th century. It took almost 200 years to show that germs make people sick! Scientists build upon the work of other scientists.

Today, newspapers, TV, and the Internet hurry to report science news. People want to hear about possible cures and discoveries. Scientists, though, depend on research published in magazines written specially for them. They know that this research has been tested. Scientists know that some information from newspapers, TV, and the Internet is wrong or incomplete.

Students must be careful when they search for information on the Internet because some of it might be wrong.

Using New Tools

Scientists use tools to find things and increase our five senses. The planet Jupiter sparkles like a star. You can see it in the night sky. The newly invented telescope, however, let the scientist Galileo Galilei take a closer look. In 1610, he found four moons around the planet! In the 17th century, that was quite a discovery!

Today, scientists have many

A replica of Galileo's telescope is in Florence, Italy.

Scientific study of the universe is exciting.

new tools. Some let us see and hear far into the sky. Others let us explore deep down in the ocean. Still others let us examine inside the human body and brain. It is exciting! Scientists continue to learn and show us more about the worlds around us.

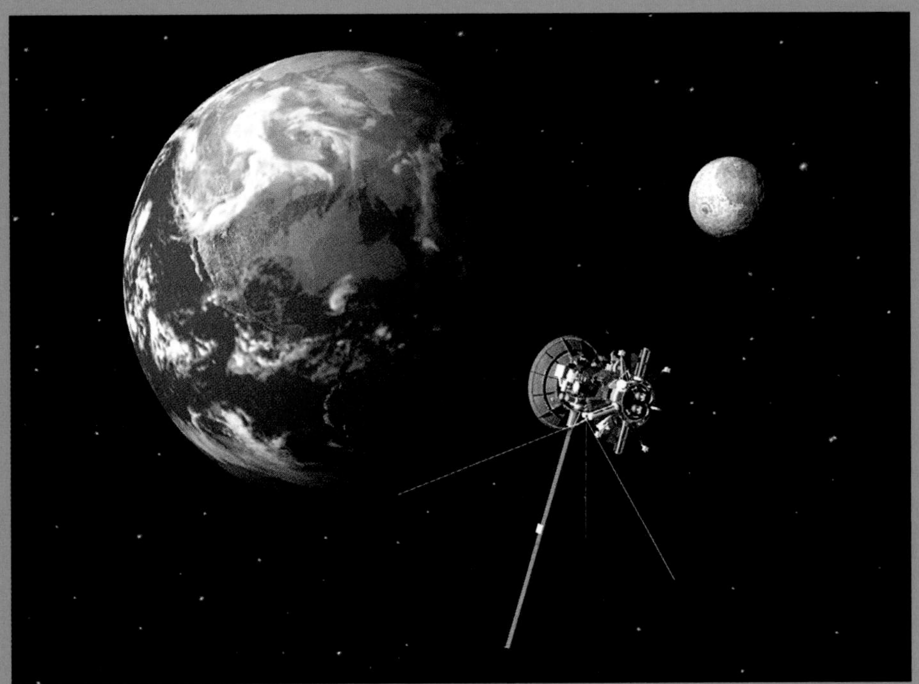

Glossary

bar graph—a visual way of comparing two or more things

conclusion—the answer a scientist gets from the results of an experiment

control group—in an experiment, the group that does not have the variable being tested

evidence—information gathered during an experiment or investigation

hypothesis—something that is suggested as being true for the purpose of further study

precautions—things done before an event to prevent harm

research—experiments and the information gathered from them

superstition—a foolish belief based on fear and the unknown

theories—based on much scientific research, these ideas explain how or why events happen

Did You Know?

- Measurements are not always exact. The first measurement of "one foot" really was the length of a man's foot. But some people have longer feet than others!

Want to Know More?

At the Library

Kramer, Stephen P. *How to Think Like a Scientist.* New York: Thomas Y. Crowell, 1987.

Swanson, Diane. *Nibbling on Einstein's Brain: The Good, the Bad, and the Bogus in Science.* Toronto: Annick Press, 2001.

Voth, Danna. *Kidsource Science Fair Handbook.* Chicago: Lowell House, 1998.

On the Web

For more information on ***how scientists work,*** use FactHound to track down Web sites related to this book.

1. Go to *www.compasspointbooks.com/facthound*
2. Type in this book ID: 0756505968
3. Click on the *Fetch It* button.

Your trusty FactHound will fetch the best Web sites for you!

Through the Mail

National Museum of Natural History
10th Street and Constitution Avenue N.W.
Washington, DC 20560
Disroom@nmnh.si.edu
To receive information about exhibits at this Smithsonian Institution museum, especially the "hands on" discovery room

On the Road

The Lawrence Hall of Science
University of California-Berkeley
Berkeley, CA 94720
510/642-5102
To visit its "Idea Laboratory," where you can use the scientific method to examine objects

Index

About the Author

Natalie M. Rosinsky writes about science, economics, history, and other fun things. One of her two cats usually sits on her computer as she works in Mankato, Minnesota. Natalie earned graduate degrees from the University of Wisconsin and has been a high school and college teacher.